99
PRAYERS
for
When You Feel
Alone

Carey Scott

BARBOUR
PUBLISHING

ISBN 978-1-64352-960-8

Published by Barbour Publishing, Inc., 1810 Barbour Drive, Uhrichsville, Ohio 44683, www.barbourbooks.com

Our mission is to inspire the world with the life-changing message of the Bible.

 Member of the
Evangelical Christian
Publishers Association

Printed in the United States of America.

Introduction

Everyone battles loneliness from time to time. It's part of the human condition that knits us together. But when those alone feelings become overwhelming, what you do next can make a big difference. God's constant message to you is a reminder of your value. You're an important part of the world today and He has designed a plan for your life. Let this book be a guide as you talk to the Lord about the condition of your heart and receive His encouragement.

Remember that isolation and loneliness are the enemy's tools to derail you, which is why God created you to thrive in community. Even more, in those seasons where you feel alone, He promises to meet you in them to renew your sense of belonging. Watch how God faithfully meets you in the pages of this book. Friend, you were never meant to navigate this life alone.

1

Not Alone

God, I am so afraid to be alone. It's an empty feeling that follows me around all day and keeps my heart anxious and unsettled. I know You say that You're always here with me, but sometimes I struggle to feel it. Would You please give me the eyes and ears to recognize Your presence in my day? Would You please strengthen me with the bold confidence to believe that I am deeply loved by You?

So don't be afraid. I am here, with you;
don't be dismayed, for I am your God. I will
strengthen you, help you. I am here with My
right hand to make right and to hold you up.
ISAIAH 41:10 VOICE

2

Thrive in Community

God, too often I hide from community because I'm intimidated by those around me, like I'm not good enough to be a part of the group. I struggle to feel like I fit in. Your Word challenges me to be strong and courageous, but that's the last thing I believe about myself. Please build my confidence to reach out and connect. Help me trust that with You by my side, I can create community and thrive in it.

"Be strong. Take courage. Don't be intimidated. Don't give them a second thought because God, your God, is striding ahead of you. He's right there with you. He won't let you down; he won't leave you."

DEUTERONOMY 31:6 MSG

3

With You Every Day

God, what a gift to know that no matter what happens in my life You are with me always. When the hard times hit, You'll be by my side as I walk through them. In my grief, fear, anger, and hurt, I can always count on Your presence. And in those times where my family and friends are unavailable, I can rest knowing Your calendar is always clear for me. Thank You for being a constant companion.

"And never forget that I am with you every day, even to the completion of this age."

MATTHEW 28:20 TPT

4

Never Abandoned

God, I feel abandoned by those I thought would always have my back. Would You please heal my heart? And Lord, thank You for promising to never walk away from me. Although it's hard sometimes, I'm choosing to believe You'll never abandon me when I need You most. As I look back, I recognize Your perfect track record in my life. So from today forward I will fully and completely trust Your Word.

You've always been right there for me; don't turn your back on me now. Don't throw me out, don't abandon me; you've always kept the door open. My father and mother walked out and left me, but God took me in.

PSALM 27:9–10 MSG

5

The Need for Companionship

God, I love that You realized Adam needed a companion. From the very beginning, You created us to be in community because You recognized our desire as humans to belong. Right now, I'm missing companionship. I'm feeling so alone and struggling to feel wanted or appreciated by those around me. Would You bring people into my life that are perfectly suited for me? I trust You to meet that need and fill that void.

It is not good for the man to be alone,
so I will create a companion for him,
a perfectly suited partner.

GENESIS 2:18 VOICE

6

He Will Take Them

God, in those times where I don't feel like anyone is willing or able to help me navigate the storms of life, I'm so thankful You always are. It's hard to walk these out on my own because they're so emotionally charged. But the Word says I can put every single worry or stress I'm feeling onto Your shoulders because You care for me so deeply. Thanks for not leaving it to me to figure out myself.

Pour out all your worries and stress upon him and leave them there, for he always tenderly cares for you.

1 Peter 5:7 tpt

7

Always Near

God, it's so rare to find people who will journey with me through the valley of darkness. I know people are busy and have their own lives to live, but I also know You made us for community. Thank You for never being too busy for me. Your love sustains me and pushes loneliness aside. I'm certain that no matter what I'm up against, You will always be near. What a gift and blessing!

Lord, even when your path takes me through the valley of deepest darkness, fear will never conquer me, for you already have! You remain close to me and lead me through it all the way. Your authority is my strength and my peace. The comfort of your love takes away my fear. I'll never be lonely, for you are near.

PSALM 23:4 TPT

8

The Wound of Rejection

God, I am struggling with rejection. My heart is wounded from people walking out of my life. It makes me feel like a throw-away person, unworthy of love. But the Bible paints a different picture, telling me I am highly valued. It says You care about my broken heart and promise to heal my pain and comfort my spirit. Thank You for picking up the pieces every time my heart is shattered.

He heals the brokenhearted and binds up their wounds [healing their pain and comforting their sorrow].

PSALM 147:3 AMP

9

Craving Community

God, thank You for knowing my deepest desires and longings. It does my weary heart so much good to realize I am actually seen and known. And I appreciate that You understand my craving for community. I need people in my life that not only love You, but also want to grow a friendship with me. It's so heavy on my heart right now. Help me trust You'll bring the right people at the right time.

Lord, you know all my desires and deepest longings. My tears are liquid words and you can read them all.

PSALM 38:9 TPT

10

He Cares for You

God, I am certain that no matter what season of life I'm in You will take care of me. I'll never be left alone to fend for myself because You promise to meet me right where I'm at. You promise to comfort those who feel alone, which is me so often. And when I choose to keep my eyes on You and trust Your ways over mine, I can always trust that You will be my Savior and Provider.

*The True God who inhabits sacred space is a
father to the fatherless, a defender of widows.
He makes a home for those who are alone. He
frees the prisoners and leads them to prosper. Yet
those who rebel against Him live in the barren
land without His blessings and prosperity.*

Psalm 68:5–6 voice

11

Never Separated from God

God, while I may feel separated from others, what a relief to know nothing will come between us. I realize how fragile my human connections can be from time to time, leaving a hole in my heart. So it's a deep sigh of relief to know I'll never be without Your hand in my life. Even when I mess up or try to hide, You see me and love me and promise to never walk away.

So who can separate us? What can come between us and the love of God's Anointed? Can troubles, hardships, persecution, hunger, poverty, danger, or even death? The answer is, absolutely nothing.

ROMANS 8:35 VOICE

12

Feeling Alone in the Battle

God, the battles are so strong right now and I don't have one person standing with me. My friendships are in turmoil, and many have turned away from me. I am scared as I walk out this challenging time alone. I am asking that You come closer so I can feel Your presence and peace. I am full of sorrow and cry out for You to comfort me as only You can.

Sorrows fill my heart as I feel helpless,
mistreated—I'm all alone and in misery!
Come closer to me now, Lord, for I need your mercy.

PSALM 25:16 TPT

13

Loneliness in Doing the Right Thing

God, it's hard to stand up for what's right because it alienates me from others. When they disagree or find me too prudish, they walk away. They desert me. But I want to live a righteous life regardless, and if I have to go it alone at times, then so be it. Will You bolster my confidence and courage, and will You remind me that You'll strengthen me and stand by me in my pursuit?

No one took my side at my first court hearing. Everyone deserted me. I hope that God doesn't hold it against them! But the Lord stood by me and gave me strength, so that the entire message would be preached through me and so all the nations could hear it. I was also rescued from the lion's mouth!

2 TIMOTHY 4:16–17 CEB

14

Never Walk Off

God, I'm choosing to trust that You won't walk away from me. I am so imperfect and make bad choices on the regular. Sometimes I worry I will finally do the one thing that makes You give up on me. I know Your Word promises You're with me forever, but I need a reminder today that my bad choices won't drive You away. I can't bear the thought of losing You as my Lord and Savior.

"God, simply because of who he is, is not going to walk off and leave his people. God took delight in making you into his very own people."

1 SAMUEL 12:22 MSG

15

Joyful Expectation
of Friendship

God, I am feeling so isolated these days and desperate for a good friend. There have been many I've enjoyed in the past, but none of them stayed for long. But I am trusting that You have someone in mind, a person who will be perfect for me. Until that time, please fill the emptiness inside of my heart and give me a joyful expectation for the amazing friend that's right around the corner.

*Some friendships don't last for long, but
there is one loving friend who is joined to
your heart closer than any other!*
PROVERBS 18:24 TPT

16

Connections in the Workplace

God, help me find connections in my job. I am
nervous about making friends and impressing
my boss at the same time. I know what it feels
like to be an island in an office setting, and I am
asking You to connect me in new and fresh ways.
Your Word says You march before me, so I am
asking that You clear the way for me to be liked
and appreciated in my workplace.

*"But the LORD is the one who is marching
before you! He is the one who will be with you!
He won't let you down. He won't abandon you.
So don't be afraid or scared!"*

DEUTERONOMY 31:8 CEB

17
Being Alone versus Lonely

God, would You help me remember that sometimes being alone is a good thing. I default to the idea that if I'm not with people all the time, I am lonely. But through scripture, Jesus proved that stealing away to spend time with You is not only good for the soul, but necessary. Give me wisdom to know when I am truly lonely and when being alone is warranted. I don't always know the difference.

Jesus repeatedly left the crowds, though, stealing away into the wilderness to pray.

LUKE 5:16 VOICE

18

Financial Outlier

God, sometimes I feel like an outlier because I can't keep up financially with my friends. They have more money and I have to decline invitations based on my budget. Your Word says to be relaxed with what I have and not be obsessed with getting more, but it's hard when my lack of funds keeps me separate. Remind me in those times when I can't participate because of money that Your presence is more than enough.

Don't be obsessed with getting more material things. Be relaxed with what you have. Since God assured us, "I'll never let you down, never walk off and leave you."

HEBREWS 13:5 MSG

19

Battling Temptation Alone

God, so often I feel alone battling temptation. I'm ashamed to share my struggles with community, afraid of being judged. I long for a support group to walk with me, but am scared to let anyone in. I know You see the complexity of my heart and have already made a path to freedom. You are so good to me. Would You give me courage to open up to a trusted friend?

Any temptation you face will be nothing new. But God is faithful, and He will not let you be tempted beyond what you can handle. But He always provides a way of escape so that you will be able to endure and keep moving forward.

1 CORINTHIANS 10:13 VOICE

20

He Will Never Turn Away from You

God, I know that even when it feels like You aren't there, You are. Even when it seems my prayers are bouncing off the ceiling, they aren't. Bolster my confidence to know there is nothing that will make You turn from me. You'll never leave me to be alone.

At three, Jesus cried out with a loud shout, "Eloi, eloi, lama sabachthani," which means, "My God, my God, why have you left me?"

MARK 15:34 CEB

21

The Wise Friend

God, help me be the kind of woman to welcome wise counsel from a friend. I have been too quick to dismiss their care and it's broken our trust. Teach me to value community so I don't walk through life alone.

The heart is delighted by the fragrance of oil and sweet perfumes, and in just the same way, the soul is sweetened by the wise counsel of a friend.

PROVERBS 27:9 VOICE

22

Restoring Community

God, thanks for always being here for me. Even when I'm wrong or selfish in my ways, You never walk away. Right now I'm feeling a little beat up by some people, and it's a lonely place to be. I know I'm not perfect, but I don't deserve to be ostracized. Help bring healing and give me a willing spirit to work through our differences. You made me for community so please help restore it.

So what should we say about all of this? If God is on our side, then tell me: whom should we fear?

ROMANS 8:31 VOICE

23

Lonely in the Unexpected

God, I admit I didn't see this coming. I was comfortable and secure, but this unexpected change has thrown me, and I have no option but to navigate this on my own. I know You've commanded me to be strong and courageous in times like this. And I know You promise to never leave me to figure it out by myself. Right now, I need reminding. I need to know You are right by my side as I find my way.

"Haven't I commanded you? Strength! Courage! Don't be timid; don't get discouraged. GOD, your God, is with you every step you take."

JOSHUA 1:9 MSG

24

Craving His Presence
through Divorce

God, I never thought my marriage would end in divorce. I've been left alone and I'm heartbroken. I've tried to comfort myself in unhealthy ways that have left me feeling emptier than before. I need You to strengthen me instead. I need to experience Your presence every minute of every day. Please don't leave me all alone. More than anything, I am asking for Your comfort to make me feel held.

I look up to the mountains; does my strength come from mountains? No, my strength comes from GOD, who made heaven, and earth, and mountains.

PSALM 121:1–2 MSG

25

The Desire to Belong

God, I have a deep longing to be known and seen. And I want to feel I belong rather than be invisible. Even more, it would be such a blessing for someone to pursue knowing me. Your Word says all of these desires are met by You. It says You know exactly who I am down to the smallest detail. Let that be enough. And if I find companionship here on earth, let it be icing on the cake.

O Eternal One, You have explored my heart and know exactly who I am; You even know the small details like when I take a seat and when I stand up again. Even when I am far away, You know what I'm thinking.

PSALM 139:1–2 VOICE

26

Comforting the Lonely

God, would You give me the spiritual eyes and ears for the lonely? I know what it feels like to be all alone, and I also know how it encourages a heart to be seen. You've been faithful to comfort me throughout my messy seasons. Let me be that kind of support for others. Equip me to comfort the lonely in their moments of need so they can experience Your love when they need it the most.

He always comes alongside us to comfort us in every suffering so that we can come alongside those who are in any painful trial. We can bring them this same comfort that God has poured out upon us.

2 Corinthians 1:4 tpt

27

That Let-Down Feeling

God, I am struggling with people letting me down. I guess I thought I had a caring and compassionate community surrounding me, but I'm realizing I don't. They let me down when I need them the most, and it's a horribly lonely feeling. I'm relieved to know Your Word says You're a proven help in times of trouble, always available. Would You surround me right now so I can find peace and comfort in Your company?

God, you're such a safe and powerful place to find refuge! You're a proven help in time of trouble—more than enough and always available whenever I need you.

PSALM 46:1 TPT

28

God Understands
Your Loneliness

God, it does my heart good to know You can relate to my loneliness. Sometimes it's really hard to open up to others about my struggles because I worry about rejection or judgment. I feel silly and shameful. So thank You for sharing Your feelings in the Bible. It brings comfort knowing I am not alone in my pain. And I appreciate that I don't even have to unpack my feelings. You know because You have felt the same way too.

He was despised and avoided by others; a man who suffered, who knew sickness well. Like someone from whom people hid their faces, he was despised, and we didn't think about him.

Isaiah 53:3 CEB

29

The Isolation of an Empty Nest

God, my heart is aching in this empty nest of a home. I miss having a house full of people I love and it's such an isolating feeling. While I'm glad they have launched and are living their best lives, it doesn't take the loneliness away. Thank You for reminding me I am not alone, because You are with me. You'll fill in the gaps left by others. Together we will figure out a new normal.

Be aware that a time is coming when you will be scattered like seeds. You will return to your own way, and I will be left alone. But I will not be alone, because the Father will be with Me.

John 16:32 voice

30

A Widow's Hope in God

God, I'm in deep grief over the loss of my spouse and my heart feels like it's going to burst. For so long, he was a constant companion and now he's gone. Thank You for being a safe place to share my needs. It helps me feel confident that I can safely put my hope in You. And thank You for wanting to hear every one of my prayers because it makes me realize I am not alone.

A widow who is truly needy and all alone puts her hope in God and keeps on going with requests and prayers, night and day.

1 TIMOTHY 5:5 CEB

31

Speaking Truth

God, it's hard to stand for what's right and speak truth because it often alienates me. It rocks the boat and causes stress and strife. In Your Word, You talk about being with me when I am facing stormy seas and raging rivers. Would You please infuse me with confidence in knowing I am loved by You and courage to stand in my convictions? I need to know I am not alone.

When you face stormy seas I will be there with you with endurance and calm; you will not be engulfed in raging rivers. If it seems like you're walking through fire with flames licking at your limbs, keep going; you won't be burned.

ISAIAH 43:2 VOICE

32

Hiding from Change

God, I am struggling with change in my life. I like predictability and stability, but that's not what I'm dealing with right now. It feels chaotic and makes me want to tuck away and hide because I'm nervous. Rather than ask for help, I navigate it alone. Because You created me and the plans for my life, I'm asking for the peace that comes with it. Help that be a touchstone every time I face unexpected change.

"For I know the plans I have for you," says the
Eternal, "plans for peace, not evil, to give you
a future and hope—never forget that."

JEREMIAH 29:11 VOICE

33

Isolated in Shame

God, I'm self-isolating because of my shame, firmly believing who I am isn't okay. I've done some horrible things in my past that's kept me from forgiving myself. And I'm worried they will keep me from Your love. But then I read in the Bible that nothing—not even shame—can come between us and it provides a glimmer of hope. Would You firm up this truth in my heart so I can thrive in community, unashamed?

*For I have every confidence that nothing—
not death, life, heavenly messengers, dark
spirits, the present, the future, spiritual powers,
height, depth, nor any created thing—can come
between us and the love of God revealed in
the Anointed, Jesus our Lord.*

ROMANS 8:38–39 VOICE

34

When You Crave Relationships

God, I feel invisible. In a group of people, I feel so alone. Sometimes I wonder if anyone would notice if I was gone. I crave relationships but am nervous to reach out, afraid of being rejected. You know my troubled heart and all the ways I feel unlovable. I am asking You to intervene and grow my confidence. Would You bring me a friend? Would You help me see my value and confirm my worth?

I look to my left and right to see if there is anyone who will help, but there's no one who takes notice of me. I have no hope of escape, and no one cares whether I live or die.

PSALM 142:4 TPT

35

Separated by Insecurities

God, Your Word says I should be content with myself. That's not easy for me because I don't feel good enough. I've struggled to connect into community in meaningful ways, leaving me with deep insecurities. I want to be liked and surrounded by friends and family, so I try so hard to be what others want. Help me make peace with who You made me to be. Anchor my confidence in how You created me.

So be content with who you are, and don't put on airs. God's strong hand is on you; he'll promote you at the right time. Live carefree before God; he is most careful with you.

1 PETER 5:6–7 MSG

36

Alone on Purpose

God, sometimes I just need to be alone. It's when I connect with You. It's how I regroup. And there are times my spirit craves what only introverting can do for me. Would You affirm that truth in me, so I don't feel guilty when I say no to invitations? Help me advocate for myself when that alone time is necessary for my mental health. And in Your goodness, would You meet me in those times to restore me?

Then, after the crowd had gone,
Jesus went up to a mountaintop alone
(as He had intended from the start).
As evening descended, He stood
alone on the mountain, praying.
MATTHEW 14:23 VOICE

37
When God is Silent

God, I'm struggling with faith right now. You promise to always be with me, but You seem distant. I can't hear You over the negative voices. I cry out but You don't respond. How long will You make me wait? I need the comfort and peace only You can provide, but it eludes me. Still, I will trust You. I will choose to believe in Your goodness. In my solitude, strengthen me as I wait.

I'm hurting, Lord—will you forget me forever? How much longer, Lord? Will you look the other way when I'm in need?

PSALM 13:1 TPT

38

Alone in Your Diagnosis

God, I'm worried about my health and the treatment plan set forth by my doctor. It's scary, and I'm withdrawing from those who love me. Open my heart to let them in, overriding the fear that I will just bog them down with worry. Even more, I really need You. I'm desperate for healing and hope for the future. Surround me with peace as You comfort my anxious heart. Keep me company as I journey down this path.

He stooped down to lift me out of danger from the desolate pit I was in, out of the muddy mess I had fallen into. Now he's lifted me up into a firm, secure place and steadied me while I walk along his ascending path.

PSALM 40:2 TPT

39

All You Want and Need

God, in those moments where I feel lonely, help me remember that You are all I want and all I really need. Keep me from dwelling on what I don't have, and instead looking at all I do have in You. Shift my perspective from victim mentality to being a victor in Your Son, Jesus Christ. And remind me of my value and worth so the enemy can't attack me in those areas that are sometimes vulnerable.

You lead me with your secret wisdom.
And following you brings me into your
brightness and glory! Whom have I in
heaven but you? You're all I want! No one
on earth means as much to me as you.

Psalm 73:24–25 tpt

40

Let God Be Your Home

God, I am at odds with my family right now and it's breaking my heart. I'm trying to advocate for myself and put some healthy boundaries in place, but I'm lonely. Would You be my Home? Even knowing my family loves me, it's still a little tricky. With You though, I always feel good because Your love secures my confidence and self-worth. I feel peaceful and safe. And honestly, it's a refreshing and much-needed change.

When my skin sags and my bones get brittle, God is rock-firm and faithful. Look! Those who left you are falling apart! Deserters, they'll never be heard from again. But I'm in the very presence of God— oh, how refreshing it is! I've made Lord God my home. God, I'm telling the world what you do!

PSALM 73:26–28 MSG

41

Loneliness in Your
New Normal

God, I'm having a tough time trying to manage my new normal. While others would like to help me, this is something I need to figure out by myself. No one can do it for me. But honestly, there are times I feel so alone. Your Word says You'll meet my every need. Right now, I desperately need to feel Your presence. I need to know You're in this with me until the end.

Know this: my God will also fill every need you have according to His glorious riches in Jesus the Anointed, our Liberating King.

PHILIPPIANS 4:19 VOICE

42
Hiding Place

God, I'm feeling attacked from all sides and standing alone without anyone to protect me. It's hard to speak up to advocate for my needs, especially when it seems no one cares. Thanks for hiding me from harm and reminding me of my freedom.

You are my hiding place. You will keep me out of trouble and envelop me with songs that remind me I am free.

PSALM 32:7 VOICE

43
The Need to Connect with Others

God, when I'm embarrassed about myself and feel exposed, I hide away. It just feels safer to be alone. But honestly, community is so good for my heart and I don't want to push it away. Please boost my confidence, remind me I don't have to be perfect, and encourage me to reach out and connect.

You're beautiful from head to toe, my dear love, beautiful beyond compare, absolutely flawless.

SONG OF SOLOMON 4:7 MSG

44

When You Want to Hide Out

God, I feel so hopeless. I'm not sure how things will ever work out, and I am worried nothing will change. In my discouragement, I just want to hide out at home. I don't want to connect with community because they don't seem to understand the complexity of my emotions. Would You give me rest? Would You be my companion during this time? Only You can make me whole again and restore my joy.

The Eternal is my shepherd, He cares for me always. He provides me rest in rich, green fields beside streams of refreshing water. He soothes my fears; He makes me whole again, steering me off worn, hard paths to roads where truth and righteousness echo His name.

PSALM 23:1–3 VOICE

45
When Church Feels Lonely

God, every Sunday I sit in church and feel completely alone. I've volunteered countless hours and joined small groups, but I don't feel like I belong. I am discouraged to not be more connected and it makes me afraid to put myself out there again. What's wrong with me? You promise hope for the weary, and I'm asking You for help. I need restoration and healing. I need grace for the journey. I need to know I'm lovable.

"Are you tired? Worn out? Burned out on religion? Come to me. Get away with me and you'll recover your life. I'll show you how to take a real rest. Walk with me and work with me—watch how I do it. Learn the unforced rhythms of grace. I won't lay anything heavy or ill-fitting on you. Keep company with me and you'll learn to live freely and lightly."
MATTHEW 11:28–30 MSG

46

The Isolation of Guilt

God, the guilt I'm carrying is so heavy. I feel like I'm falling into a deep pit of despair all by myself, too embarrassed to open up and share my struggle. I'm worried about being judged. So what a relief to know You'll keep me from slipping away. You will hold me when I'm ashamed to let others in. You'll bring peace when I need it. And You will remove the guilty feelings that keep me isolated.

If GOD hadn't been there for me, I never would have made it. The minute I said, "I'm slipping, I'm falling," your love, GOD, took hold and held me fast. When I was upset and beside myself, you calmed me down and cheered me up.

PSALM 94:17–19 MSG

47

When You Can't Trust Anyone Else

God, I feel so betrayed by those I thought cared deeply for me. I feel as though I have no one whom I can trust. My heart is broken, and I'm angry, and I need Your comfort. Even more, I'm craving Your presence because I can't trust anyone else right now. The Bible says You're always available when needed. Right now, please flood my heart with comfort, companionship, and peace.

Behold, I stand at the door and knock;
if anyone hears and listens to and heeds
My voice and opens the door, I will come
in to him and will eat with him,
and he [will eat] with Me.

REVELATION 3:20 AMPC

48

Unmet Needs in Motherhood

God, I am struggling as a mom. I'm exhausted and feeling isolated from the things I want to do. It feels like my desires don't matter because everything is centered around the kids. Honestly, most of the time I want to lock myself in the closet and cry. The Word describes You as a shelter and fortress, and I am trusting You to care for and protect my weary heart. Please be with me.

He who takes refuge in the shelter of the Most High will be safe in the shadow of the Almighty. He will say to the Eternal, "My shelter, my mighty fortress, my God, I place all my trust in You."

PSALM 91:1–2 VOICE

49

Inflated Feelings of Loneliness

God, when I feel unimportant to others, I tend to detach to avoid the hurt. I disconnect because it makes my heart feel safer. And doing so inflates my feelings of loneliness tenfold. I love that scripture says You've written my name on Your hand. It's a powerful reminder You will never walk away. And even when I feel unloved and unvalued by those around me, I'm thankful to know I matter to You.

"Can a mother forget the infant at her breast, walk away from the baby she bore? But even if mothers forget, I'd never forget you—never. Look, I've written your names on the backs of my hands. The walls you're rebuilding are never out of my sight."

ISAIAH 49:15–16 MSG

50

When No One Seems to Care

God, I have no one else to comfort me but You.
My heart is broken and I'm weary, struggling on
so many levels. It seems like no one cares about
the battles I've been facing, because my support
system has disappeared. I thought I was more
loved. Today's verse is spot on for how I'm feeling, and I'm bringing my hurts to You because
I know You care. Please wrap Your Daddy arms
around me right now.

I'm depressed, lonely, forgotten, and abandoned.
I'm sleepless, shivering in the cold, forlorn and
friendless, like a lonely bird on the rooftop.

PSALM 102:6–7 TPT

Companionship in
Your Calling

God, You designed me with a call on my life and scripture says I have a hope and a future. I know I'll need Your wisdom and companionship to walk it out because my ability will come from You. What a privilege to journey together! Thank You for knowing it could be lonely, and for filling that gap through the Holy Spirit living in my heart. I look forward to deepening our relationship in new and fresh ways.

"And I will ask the Father and he will give you another Savior, the Holy Spirit of Truth, who will be to you a friend just like me—and he will never leave you. The world won't receive him because they can't see him or know him. But you will know him intimately, because he will make his home in you and will live inside you."

John 14:16–17 tpt

52

Watching and Listening for God

God, when I feel like no one else will help me, I believe You will. I'm asking You to be tangible in my troubling situation and lead me down the path to freedom. I don't know the right way to go. I'm watching and listening for You!

I look to my left and right to see if there is anyone who will help, but there's no one who takes notice of me. I have no hope of escape, and no one cares whether I live or die.
PSALM 142:4 TPT

53

Belonging and Being Loved

God, You're my safe place. More than any other person I trust, I am placing my broken heart in Your hands. Replace my loneliness with joy and my hopelessness with peace. Your presence makes me feel like I belong and am fiercely loved.

You are the One I called to, O Eternal One. I said, "You're the only safe place I know; You're all I've got in this world."
PSALM 142:5 VOICE

54
Lonely in the Day-To-Day

God, sometimes I feel lonely in the day-to-day, mundane tasks in my life. It's the same thing over and over again. From meal planning to bill paying to calendar keeping, it's easy to lose my purpose and passion. I stop seeking Your direction as I get lost in the humdrum. Your Word says scripture empowers, instructs, corrects, and directs. It breathes new life into old bones. Thank You for being with me and seeing my needs.

Every Scripture has been written by the Holy Spirit, the breath of God. It will empower you by its instruction and correction, giving you the strength to take the right direction and lead you deeper into the path of godliness.

2 TIMOTHY 3:16 TPT

55

The Promises in Separation

God, from the beginning You set me apart and gave me instructions to live a holy life. You didn't ask me to sit in judgment of others, but to instead keep myself from the party atmosphere where bad choices often happen. You promised to meet my needs for community, giving me a place to feel I belong. And while this has been hard at times, You've kept Your word and I am finding connection. Thank You!

I never joined the party crowd in their laughter and their fun. Led by you, I went off by myself. You'd filled me with indignation. Their sin had me seething.

JEREMIAH 15:17 MSG

56

The Emptiness of Grief

God, my heart is full of sadness and my spirit is crushed. I'm grieving the loss of someone I loved very much, and I can't believe they are gone. There is a huge hole in my heart that no one can fill, except You. Please surround me with Your grace and love. Show me the path to healing. Be my companion as I walk this path of mourning. I'm desperate for hope, and long for Your company.

A heart full of joy and goodness makes a cheerful face, but when a heart is full of sadness the spirit is crushed.

PROVERBS 15:13 AMP

57
No Place or Space

God, it's good for my heart to know there is no place or space that separates me from You. I can't sin too much to make You leave or work too hard to lose Your attention. You promise to be with me always and I can bank on it. Help me remember this when I feel all alone. Keep my heart from buying into lies of abandonment. Let me feel Your presence in those lonely times.

Where could I go from your Spirit? Where could I run and hide from your face? If I go up to heaven, you're there! If I go down to the realm of the dead, you're there too!

PSALM 139:7–8 TPT

58

A God Who Understands

God, sometimes it's difficult to speak out about my value system and what beliefs I hold dear. So many people around me believe differently, and I often feel judged for those differences. I get nervous to share my thoughts because I don't want to alienate myself even more. So instead, I stay quiet and alone. Thank You for knowing the depths of my heart and grounding me in Truth. I am grateful to always have You.

But you, God, shield me on all sides; You ground my feet, you lift my head high; With all my might I shout up to God, His answers thunder from the holy mountain.

PSALM 3:3–4 MSG

59

The Good Side of Alone

God, thank You for today's verse that reminds me there are times it's okay to send people away and be alone. It's not being disrespectful or mean-spirited. Instead, it's advocating for myself. There is purpose in alone-time. Help me know when it's important to be part of community and when it's time to retreat. And give me the confidence to do what is best for me so I can be my best for others.

Later that afternoon the disciples came to Jesus and said, "It's going to be dark soon and the people are hungry, but there's nothing to eat here in this desolate place. You should send the crowds away to the nearby villages to buy themselves some food."
MATTHEW 14:15 TPT

60

God's Companionship

God, there is no one who can comfort me like You. So often it feels like I have nobody who cares for me in the ways You do. When I look for compassion from those around me, I'm left discouraged because their efforts fall short. I'm not a priority and it's hurtful. But You never disappoint me when I need help. You respond to every tear and plea. And Your companionship means everything to me.

When the upright need help and cry to the Eternal, He hears their cries and rescues them from all of their troubles.

PSALM 34:17 VOICE

61

God Understands

God, it never occurred to me that You would understand the feeling of loneliness. I mean, You're God! But it must have been lonely when Your One and only Son died on the cross. In that moment, the two of You were disconnected. Your closest companion was gone. I'm so grateful there is nothing I can walk through that You haven't experienced. You're so loving and caring, and it's a privilege to be Your child.

"God so loved the world that he gave his only Son, so that everyone who believes in him won't perish but will have eternal life."

JOHN 3:16 CEB

62

The Precedent of Replacing

God, I need a friend. My bestie walked away from our relationship and I am battling feelings of abandonment. I've been rejected by someone I thought would always be with me. And because You've set a precedent of replacing people of importance, I'm asking You to honor my request. Would You bless me with another good friend? I don't want to walk through life all by myself. Thank You for being faithful to Your children.

"And I will ask the Father and he will give you another Savior, the Holy Spirit of Truth, who will be to you a friend just like me— and he will never leave you."

JOHN 14:16 TPT

63

The Benefit of Isolating with God

God, I'm grateful for the example set by today's verse. It's easy to feel vulnerable when I'm alone, so I never choose to be. Instead, I fill my calendar with people. But I'm learning about the power that comes from being alone with You in prayer. I'm understanding the necessity of isolating with You for restoration. And I am changing my perspective on alone-time because I'm seeing the benefit of it.

The next morning, Jesus got up long before daylight, left the house while it was dark, and made his way to a secluded place to give himself to prayer.

MARK 1:35 TPT

64

Grappling Alone in Grief

God, how much longer will I have to grapple with my grief alone? I've cried out for Your relief, but my heart is still heavy with pain. I have no one to walk me through this heartbreak except You and I'm desperate to hear Your voice. Bring the peace of Jesus. Comfort my anxiousness. Give me strength to not lose hope. And please guide me safely to the other side of grief.

How much longer must I cling to this constant grief? I've endured this shaking of my soul. So how much longer will my enemy have the upper hand? It's been long enough!

PSALM 13:2 TPT

65

He Never Leaves Your Side

God, when I start counting the number of prayers You've answered, I realize I'm not as alone as I sometimes feel. You have been so faithful to respond to my pleas for help; I can't think of a time You weren't there for me. In those seasons where my human community feels sparse, please remind me that my heavenly Father has never left my side. The revelation of Your faithfulness fills my heart!

I've thrown myself headlong into your arms—
I'm celebrating your rescue. I'm singing at the top
of my lungs, I'm so full of answered prayers.
PSALM 13:5–6 MSG

66

Replenishing from Rejection

God, it refreshes my soul to draw near to You. When I'm feeling rejected or abandoned at work, I look forward to coming home to connect with You. It gives me something to look forward to after a rough day, and it replaces those lonely feelings with hope. Your presence fills my love bucket so I can navigate the workplace once again. Thank You for being my refuge and safe place. I couldn't do it without You!

But it is good for me to draw near to God; I have put my trust in the Lord God and made Him my refuge, that I may tell of all Your works.

PSALM 73:28 AMPC

67

When You Self-Isolate

God, I'm struggling with wanting to isolate because I don't want to burden anyone with my stuff. So often I feel like I need to handle things on my own. I worry about inconveniencing others or being judged. It's not that I don't want community or that I only care about myself, but more because I lack confidence. Help me remember that friends and family are a gift, and we are meant to help one another.

An unfriendly person isolates himself and seems to care only about his own issues. For his contempt of sound judgment makes him a recluse.

PROVERBS 18:1 TPT

68

Putting Yourself Out There Again

God, give me confidence to put myself out there again. I know it's important that I connect with community because it's one of the best ways to encourage and inspire one another. I need this as do those around me. And when I hide away, we all miss the goodness that friendship brings. Embolden me to reach out to others. Empower me with bravery to be myself. And open my heart to new friends and situations.

Let us consider how to inspire each other
to greater love and to righteous deeds, not
forgetting to gather as a community, as some
have forgotten, but encouraging each other,
especially as the day of His return approaches.
HEBREWS 10:24–25 VOICE

69

Keeping Good Company

God, I know the importance of hanging out with the right people. The solution to my loneliness isn't filling the emptiness unwisely. Instead, I need to make good choices with the company I keep. Give me discernment to know whom to spend time with and whom to avoid. This isn't me being full of judgment, but rather me choosing to surround myself with those who will help me live and love well.

People will be selfish and love money. They will be the kind of people who brag and who are proud. They will slander others, and they will be disobedient to their parents. They will be ungrateful, unholy, unloving, contrary, and critical. They will be without self-control and brutal, and they won't love what is good.

2 Timothy 3:2–3 CEB

70

Alone through Illness

God, I am holding hope that I will be reunited with my family and friends soon. This illness has been a hard road and I'm missing my community. While I understand the need for temporary separation, I am so lonely. Please reunite us as soon as possible.

Build up hope so you'll all be together in this, no one left out, no one left behind. I know you're already doing this; just keep on doing it.
1 THESSALONIANS 5:11 MSG

71

Lonely from Loss

God, my heart grieves the loss of my husband. For so many years, He was my closest friend and companion and I'm missing him so much right now. Please comfort my broken heart, and please fill the empty space with Your Holy presence. I need You right now!

Two are better than one because a good return comes when two work together. If one of them falls, the other can help him up. But who will help the pitiful person who falls down alone?
ECCLESIASTES 4:9–10 VOICE

72

Never Really Alone

God, I would rather feel a little lonely as I stand for what's right than surround myself with people who are bad influences. I know that You promise to never leave me. So in those *alone* seasons of life, the truth is that I am not. You are with me always no matter what! And that means I can use good and sound judgment as I decide whom I will invest my time in.

Do not be so deceived and misled!
Evil companionships (communion, associations)
corrupt and deprave good manners and
morals and character.

1 CORINTHIANS 15:33 AMPC

73

Isolation in Marriage

God, when I feel lonely in my marriage and isolated from sharing our struggles with others, remind me I have You to talk to. Be my companion through the valleys. Infuse my heart with Your grace so I can stay engaged in my marriage as we try to work through the differences we're facing. Replace my weakness with Your strength and fill me with hope. And saturate the emptiness with Your goodness.

He said to me, "My grace is enough for you,
because power is made perfect in weakness."
So I'll gladly spend my time bragging about my
weaknesses so that Christ's power can rest on me.
2 Corinthians 12:9 CEB

74
Purposeful Separation

God, sometimes the best thing I can do is separate myself from a situation. When it's all hitting the fan and tempers are flaring, give me wisdom and courage to know when to take a step back. It may feel lonely to do so, but there are times we all need space to process. Help me remember this loneliness is temporary and necessary. And meet me in the isolation so I know You're with me.

Go, my people, enter your rooms and shut your doors behind you. Take cover, for in a little while the fury will be over.

ISAIAH 26:20 CEB

75

Yes, You Belong!

God, today's verse is such an awesome reminder that I belong. I have a place in the body of Christ and am a vital part of something meaningful. When I forget that truth is when loneliness really sets in. So please bring this powerful fact to my mind when I begin to entertain the thought that I don't fit in anywhere. The reality is that I do. Even more, I'm a unique and unmatched part of Your body!

You are the body of the Anointed One,
and each of you is a unique and vital part of it.

1 CORINTHIANS 12:27 TPT

76
Count It As Joy?

God, Your Word says to consider every test and trial as an occasion for joy. And if true, it means I should ask You to reveal the bigger picture when I feel alone because it's an opportunity for growth and maturity. Rather than sit and sulk, I want perspective. Give me Your strength and joy to infiltrate the loneliness. And help me remember that You'll never leave nor forsake me, so I'm never actually alone!

My brothers and sisters, think of the various tests you encounter as occasions for joy. After all, you know that the testing of your faith produces endurance. Let this endurance complete its work so that you may be fully mature, complete, and lacking in nothing.

JAMES 1:2–4 CEB

77

The Courage to Be a Doer

God, the Word says to be a doer and not only a hearer. It's hard to walk that out when I close myself off from community. I struggle to feel good about who I am which keeps me from confidently engaging with others. What if I'm rejected as I try to love? What if I'm judged for speaking truth? Sometimes it just feels safer to be alone. Please give me courage to be a doer. I need Your help.

You must be doers of the word and not only hearers who mislead themselves. Those who hear but don't do the word are like those who look at their faces in a mirror. They look at themselves, walk away, and immediately forget what they were like.

JAMES 1:22–24 CEB

God is Intimately Aware!

God, my heart longs to be seen and known. I want to be celebrated and cherished. But it seems like a far-off hope that won't come to pass. What a treat to read today's verse because it encourages me in spades! To know You're intimately aware of me delights those lonely places inside. You know my heart, You know my words, You know my next step. I am not alone! You are with me always!

You are so intimately aware of me, Lord. You read my heart like an open book and you know all the words I'm about to speak before I even start a sentence! You know every step I will take before my journey even begins.

PSALM 139:3–4 TPT

79
Always with You

God, what a relief to know that no matter where I go You are with me. There's nothing I can do to remove Your presence from my life. So when I'm feeling isolated and abandoned, the reality is that I'm not. I may be lacking worldly community, but never Your divine company. Thanks for always knowing exactly what I need. My heart is at peace because I have You by my side.

Wherever I go, your hand will guide me; your strength will empower me. It's impossible to disappear from you or to ask the darkness to hide me, for your presence is everywhere, bringing light into my night.

PSALM 139:10–11 TPT

80

Never Unseen

God, anytime I feel unseen let me remember You know the smallest of details about me. Let me remember I'm a one-of-a-kind creation. Remind me I was made on purpose and for a purpose, and that You don't make trash. Fill my heart with the knowledge of how much I mean to You. And open my eyes to the truth that You're always with me as I navigate the ups and downs of this life.

I will offer You my grateful heart, for I am Your unique creation, filled with wonder and awe. You have approached even the smallest details with excellence; Your works are wonderful; I carry this knowledge deep within my soul.

PSALM 139:14 VOICE

81

Asking God to Uncover

God, would You search me and let me know if I am doing something to alienate others? Would You look at my heart and motives and uncover anything in me that needs readjustment? This isn't the first time I've found myself in this lonely place, and I am open to Your correction if necessary. Sharpen my eyes and ears to the truth. And give me the courage to make any changes You may reveal.

Explore me, O God, and know the real me. Dig deeply and discover who I am. Put me to the test and watch how I handle the strain. Examine me to see if there is an evil bone in me, and guide me down Your path forever.

PSALM 139:23–24 VOICE

82

The Holy Spirit

God, how can I feel alone when I realize I have the Holy Spirit living in me? Because I've accepted Jesus as my Savior, Your Spirit has now taken up residence in my body. I have a built-in friend 24-7 who promises to never leave. The Spirit is alive and active, guiding me and empowering me to live a righteous life. Let me remember His presence anytime I begin to feel lonely.

Have you forgotten that your body is now the sacred temple of the Spirit of Holiness, who lives in you? You don't belong to yourself any longer, for the gift of God, the Holy Spirit, lives inside your sanctuary.

1 Corinthians 6:19 TPT

83

God Always Notices

God, my heart is blessed to know that You come looking for those You love. Sometimes I wonder if anyone notices I am not around. Does anyone see that I'm not out and about? Am I missed? Thank You for adding this verse to Your Word because it encourages me to know You will always notice when I'm hiding. And even more, You will come looking for me because I matter to You.

But the Lord God called to Adam and said to him, Where are you?

GENESIS 3:9 AMPC

84
Kicked in the Gut

God, meet me right where I am in my sadness. I'm feeling tossed aside and uncared for and my heart is broken. I never saw this level of betrayal coming and I'm at a loss. Restore my peace and hope like only You can.

If your heart is broken, you'll find GOD right there; if you're kicked in the gut, he'll help you catch your breath.

PSALM 34:18 MSG

85
He Will Take You In

God, pull me in close to You and take this empty feeling away from me! I feel hopeless and unwanted, and I'm desperate to know that I matter. Speak kindly into my heart and remind me that I am important in Your eyes. I need to know that right now.

My father and mother abandoned me. I'm like an orphan! But you took me in and made me yours.

PSALM 27:10 TPT

86

Sin Keeps You Alone

God, thank You for freedom. Thank You for removing the chains of bondage that keep me in sin and slavery. And thank You for calling me to stand my ground. It's always a telltale sign that I'm falling back into the yoke of slavery when I choose to isolate from others. Open my eyes to see that tendency because so often I'm not aware I'm headed there. Sin keeps me alone. Freedom invites community.

Christ has set us free to live a free life.
So take your stand! Never again let
anyone put a harness of slavery on you.

GALATIANS 5:1 MSG

87

The Pitfall of Approval

God, empower me not to care so much about pleasing people that I go against what I know is true and right. In my pursuit of community, don't allow me to lose my moral compass. I don't want those lonely feelings to cause me to make the wrong choices for the approval of others. I would rather stand alone for a season with You than sacrifice our relationship to feel accepted by the wrong people. Please give me wisdom.

Do you think I care about the approval of men
or about the approval of God? Do you think
I am on a mission to please people? If I am
still spinning my wheels trying to please men,
then there is no way I can be a servant of the
Anointed One, the Liberating King.

GALATIANS 1:10 VOICE

88

Expecting Lonely Seasons

God, it helps knowing I should expect some lonely seasons. I don't want to live on the world's terms, striving for its acceptance. Instead, I want my life to reflect a relationship with Jesus. I want my words and actions to point to You in heaven. And if that means I may find myself struggling to find community every now and then, help me remember that You promise to never leave me nor forsake me.

"If you find the godless world is hating you, remember it got its start hating me. If you lived on the world's terms, the world would love you as one of its own. But since I picked you to live on God's terms and no longer on the world's terms, the world is going to hate you."

JOHN 15:18–19 MSG

God Fully Knows You

God, in those times I feel unknown, bring me back to today's verse that clearly states You've known me since before I took my first breath. Before I saw the light of day I was fully known, and my future plans had been established. You have never left my side, not for one moment. I may feel alone but the reality is that I am not. Thank You for being my constant companion, invested in my life!

"Before I shaped you in the womb, I knew all about you. Before you saw the light of day, I had holy plans for you: A prophet to the nations— that's what I had in mind for you."

JEREMIAH 1:5 MSG

90

The Company You Keep

God, I know the company I keep matters. They can either be beneficial, helping me grow and mature to become the best version possible; or they can influence me negatively and cause me to make the wrong choices that lead me away from You. Help me make the hard decisions even if that means my community may be limited, and at times leave me feeling lonely. I trust You to fill those empty spaces.

If you want to grow in wisdom, spend time with the wise. Walk with the wicked and you'll eventually become just like them.

PROVERBS 13:20 TPT

91

Because Jesus Understands

God, Your Son understands the lonely feelings better than anyone. He knows what it's like to be despised and abandoned. Jesus felt rejection. And as hard as it is to imagine Him walking this out, I deeply appreciate how relatable it makes Him. When I cry out in anguish with these same issues, it matters so much that Jesus understands. It encourages me to know that He will comfort me through them.

So he was despised and forsaken by men, this man of suffering, grief's patient friend. As if he was a person to avoid, we looked the other way; he was despised, forsaken, and we took no notice of him.

ISAIAH 53:3 VOICE

92
Whose Opinion Matters Most?

God, mature my faith so I'm able to trust who You say I am more than worrying about what others think. When I focus my attention on worldly opinions, I'm stirred up. But when I find rest in Your thoughts about me, I'm content and at peace. Give me confidence to be alone when it's the right thing to do. And when it's time, give me courage to seek community with the right people.

The fear of human opinion disables;
trusting in GOD protects you from that.
PROVERBS 29:25 MSG

93
Walking Away

God, give me the courage to walk away from the bad influences in my life. Too often, I justify staying with them because I fear loneliness more. Help me trust that You will meet my need for belonging in the perfect ways. You know my fears and insecurities, and I'm trusting that You will untangle them so I can find community in the right places.

Walk away from the company of fools,
for you cannot find insight in their words.
PROVERBS 14:7 VOICE

94
Self-Made Loneliness

God, open my eyes to see the needs of others rather than self-isolating as I fixate on my tough circumstances. Sometimes the desire to protect my own heart keeps me alone and missing out of community. Help me trust You with my brokenness so I'm still able to contribute to relationships around me in meaningful ways. I want to be ready and able to bless others rather than get locked up in my self-made prison of selfishness.

And show hospitality to strangers, for they may be angels from God showing up as your guests.
HEBREWS 13:2 TPT

God Will Meet You
in Loneliness

God, I feel mismatched in some of my relation-ships right now. There's a tension between what I know are healthy thoughts and what I'm being pressured to believe. I'm struggling with how to stand strong in truth because I'm afraid of abandonment if I go against their ideas. Please encourage my heart to stay true to Your Word, trusting that You will honor it. I don't want to be alone, but I know You'll meet me in it.

Don't continue to team up with unbelievers in mismatched alliances, for what partnership is there between righteousness and rebellion? Who could mingle light with darkness? What harmony can there be between Christ and Satan? Or what does a believer have in common with an unbeliever?

2 Corinthians 6:14–15 tpt

96

When Family Rejects

God, family is messy. And there are so many strings attached that it's easy to get tangled in expectations I can't or won't meet. Standing up for my faith often means alienation by the ones I always thought would be there for me. But none of this escapes You. In my abandonment and rejection, I know You'll be my companion. Bring other faith-honoring friends to fill the emptiness too. I trust You to meet every need!

Your own parents, brothers, relatives, and friends will turn on you and turn you in. Some of you will be killed, and all of you will be hated by everyone for the sake of My name.

LUKE 21:16–17 VOICE

97

When the Problem is You

God, maybe the reason I struggle with community is because I'm not living out today's verse in my everyday life. Maybe I am expecting to be treated one way but not treating others the same way. Father, open my eyes to the places where I am bringing about my own loneliness. Show me where I need to make changes. Help me see the ways I'm not living and loving others well. I am listening!

If you don't want to be judged, don't judge. If you don't want to be condemned, don't condemn. If you want to be forgiven, forgive.

LUKE 6:37 VOICE

Loneliness from Keeping Up

God, it's lonely trying to keep up with the Joneses. Watching my friends purchase new cars, take expensive trips, and fill their homes with the latest and greatest reminds me I can't keep up. So rather than try, I hide away in shame. Your Word says any treasures on earth are worthless and heavenly stockpiles should be my focus. That means it's okay I can't keep up with others. I'm not supposed to!

"Don't hoard treasure down here where it gets eaten by moths and corroded by rust or—worse!—stolen by burglars. Stockpile treasure in heaven, where it's safe from moth and rust and burglars. It's obvious, isn't it? The place where your treasure is, is the place you will most want to be, and end up being."

MATTHEW 6:19–21 MSG

99

The Purpose of Friendship

God, I know friends are vital to living a good life. But sometimes I toss them away when conflict arises because I don't want to deal with it. Forgive me! Maybe that's why I find myself alone so much. Your Word says conflict can be a good thing and sometimes used to sharpen character. Fill me with grace and perspective so I can deepen friendships to weather every storm.

It takes a grinding wheel to sharpen a blade,
and so one person sharpens the character of another.

PROVERBS 27:17 TPT